TROLLEY TRIPS

NEWCASTLE
TEESSIDE
READING
BOURNEMOUTH

INTRODUCTION

In the course of my work, in the 1960s, I was fortunate enough to be able to visit several English trolleybus towns. At some places I stayed a few days. At others it was only a few hours. Most of the systems were contracting – some in their final weeks of survival. The route diagrams relate to the system at the time of my visit. Here is my tribute to them.

Being a photographer, not a trolleybus expert, I haven't a clue about makes of vehicles and so on. Hopefully you will just enjoy the nostalgia of the images.

The majority of these photographs are previously unpublished, and are copyright of the author unless otherwise stated.

Thanks to author and colleague Steven Lockwood for his valuable assistance in identifying some locations for which my notes had been misplaced !

Stan Ledgard
2010

Front Cover: Bournemouth 275 on route 20 to Christchurch is seen amongst the foliage in Old Christchurch Road.

NEWCASTLE

A few days spent here in the 1960s enabled all of the remaining system to be walked. The trolleys were generally much tidier than the city seemed to be. I have a lasting memory of scruffy individuals lurking outside the railway station trying to sell condoms; of innumerable doorways occupied in the early morning by alcohol-and-urine impregnated persons, both male and female; and of long wide roads where little seemed to be happening except the occasional trolleybus humming along amid graffiti and dereliction.

The only routes which had been abandoned at this time were to Wallsend (Park Road) and to Grange Estate.

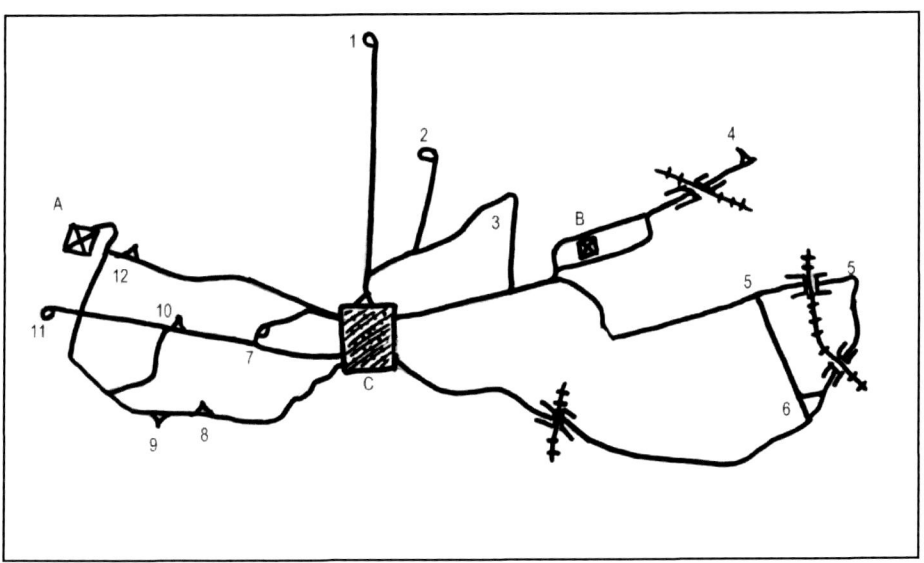

Key

A Slatyford Depot
B Byker Depot
C Town Centre
1 Gosforth Park
2 Osborne Road
3 Heaton
4 Wallsend Boundary
5 Westbourne Avenue
6 Church Street
7 Brighton Grove
8 Benwell Church
9 Delaval Road
10 Fox and Hounds
11 Denton Square
12 Fenham

527 turns in to Station Road from Church Street. The wires along Walker Road (route 34 Wallsend) have been removed.

525 disgorges her passengers at her 35C Westbourne Avenue terminus. Now she will turn right into Church Street and reverse out again. 527 has done this and returns along Welbeck Road.

621 on 35A Brighton Grove at the Church Street/Proctor Street (on the right) junction. The wires of the Walker Road/Welbeck Road link are seen tied off on the left, but the rest of Church Street is still wired.

For the final couple of years of this terminus, there were further alterations. All wires in Church St were removed. Trolleys on route 35 now approached via Proctor St, turned right on a new stub into Church St, reversed into Wharrier St (which had never had wires) then retraced their route. The frog going nowhere to the left was a relic of the previous layout.

607 completes her move at the Wallsend Boundary reverser.

Dwarfed by the industry, 450 heads for Wallsend Boundary.

629 on 35 Church Street turns from Welbeck Road into White Street, and return via Church Street. On the right, wires towards Wallsend have been removed though the frog remains.

Just a few yards up Welbeck Road is the railway bridge. 481 on 35 Denton Square leads a motorbus, followed by another trolley also on route 35.

604 for Denton Square runs along White Street passing Beal and Son, Anchor and Chain Cables supplier.

619 passes under the railway bridge near the railway station, approaching White Street.

611 has de-wired on White Street. Her conductor fishes for the booms. Several trolleys pass her (on traction batteries).

Above

586 passes by, her conductor riding on the platform carrying his bamboo.

Left

The linesmen struggle to retrieve the negative boom and replace the trolley head which has been torn off.

615, followed by a bus, crosses Byker Bridge en route for Westbourne Avenue.

583 heads for Church Street. Seen at Byker, the wires to the right are for Wallsend Boundary. The wire across the top of the photo links inbound route 35 to outbound route 32.

At Neville Street/Central Station, three passing loops provided standing for several routes: 609 is on '44 Fenham' while 622 picks up for '42 Heaton Road'.

501 on (36) makes her way past 622. The turnaround at Scotswood Road is just behind them.

Hurtling down Westgate, 606 is harlf-heartedly pursued by an AEC motorbus passing under the junction at Elswick Road.

513 slows at the bottom of Westgate as she nears the town centre.

Looking along Percy Street, 493 for '33A Osbourne Road' turns from Northumberland Street to Barras Bridge.

501 is about to cross Grainger Street. For some reason she displays route 33B instead of 35C. Who really cares?!

617 shelters amongst motorbuses at the Haymarket/Morden Street bus layover park.

580 exits Morden Street into Percy Street to take up service on '33A Deleval Road'.

586 passes Morden Street junction on route 41 Heaton Road.

622 heading for Central Station climbs Benton Bank from Heaton, as motorbus 299 descends.

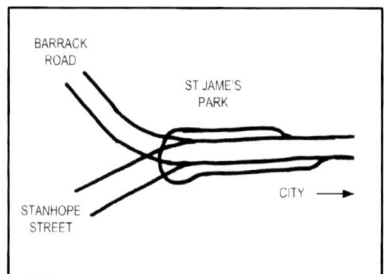

<u>Above</u>
Two unidentified trolleys cross by St James' Park, on the City-Fenham service.

The overhead layout here was a little complicated

627 showing 35B Welbeck Road runs along Stanhope Street. She will turn to her left into Dilston Road which is part of the Brighton Grove turning loop.

A trolley from Denton Square passes 'Fox and Hounds'. The reversing triangle for journeys from City is on the right. Wires going left are for routes 37/38.

494 on (35A) climbs Denton Bank with ease.

580 showing '43 Central Station' actually heads for Fenham, and is seen on Whickham View, passing Ferguson Lane.

An unidentified trolley speeds along Jesmond Road at Jesmond Dene.

At Byker Depot, 590 waits on the forecourt for her crew.

Sister 591 heads the line of trolleys awaiting the scrap man.

THE COLOUR BIT IN THE MIDDLE
NEWCASTLE

603 departs from Denton Square, leaving 596 blocked in behind a motorbus. At the time this terminus had a pleasant open aspect.

585 showing '42 Newgate Street' runs along Percy Street near the former Haymarket depot.

527 outbound trundles across Byker Bridge.

582 on the exit wires at Byker depot.

TEESSIDE

After linking Grangetown with Normanby, trolleys could still (for a while) terminate at Grangetown, or run a sort of circular. This is the new layout at Grangetown.

285 (formerly 5) runs along the newly-installed link wires, although road widening is still underway.

Sporting the new turquoise livery, 285 helped out with the final trolley weekend., seen here, turning from the 'new' link wires at Grangetown.
The terminal facility had been removed some time before.

Little-used wiring is a 'must' for trolleybus tours. 285 uses the reverser near the Whitworth Road junction.

BOURNEMOUTH

272 on route 23 negotiates The Square, heading for Old Christchurch Road.

Gervis Place near the town centre had space for four trolleys to lay over. 296 heads the line-up.

READING

Armour Hill terminus occupied by trolley 186. For some reason this loop reminds me of Thornton terminus in Bradford.

172 picks up at the cemetery on the descent from Armour Hill.

172 speeds down Park Lane from the Tilehurst terminus.

178 turns from School Road into Norcot Road, en route from Tilehurst to Wokingham Road. Note the marker lights along the overhead.

153 with her platform doors firmly closed, turns on the railway station loop.

185 is about to join Oxford Road at the roundabout at 'The Kentwood'.

TEESSIDE

The Teesside Railless Traction Board (TRTB) operated in perhaps the ugliest, smelliest area of England which was served by trolleybuses. However, the environment itself provided a unique backdrop and, if the wind was blowing to the east, some areas were almost pleasantly habitable! A couple of visits here show the complete change of livery of the fleet, from smart dark green to insipid turquoise which looked completely out of place.

The two routes (North Ormesby to Grangetown, and North Ormesby to Normanby) were latterly joined Grangetown to Normanby, giving a sort of P-shaped layout. There were intermediate turning points at Whitworth Road and at South Bank, when coming from Cargo Fleet. The overhead appeared to be generally sloppy but seemed to work okay.

Designed primarily for getting people to and from work, the system served no large town, but connected former villages, sprawling housing estates and heavy industry.

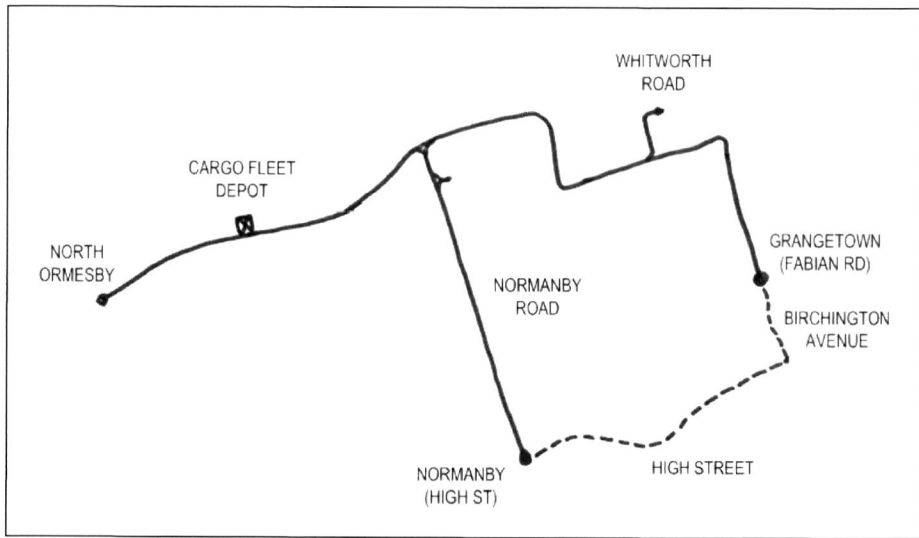

Approaching from Middlesbrough, the first sighting of TRTB trolleys was at North Ormesby. The terminus was a very tight circle at a T-junction. On the turn, trolleybuses ran against the traffic on the main road ! Number 3 turns on the circle.

Another view of the terminus, which left little room for driver error. Number 5 completes the move.

At North Ormesby, being the terminus for both routes, it was common to see two trolleys standing there. Trolley 7 waits behind a motorbus and another trolley, in the 'shopping street'.

The roads which the routes followed varied from narrow ones through heavy industry to spacious carriageways. One of the latter was encountered near the depot. No. 16 stops to pick up. The TRTB depot is on the left of the photo.

The TRTB depot for both trolleys and motorbuses was at Cargo Fleet. The wiring formed a complete circle from which one road led to the shed, reversing in being the norm. The eastbound wires from North Ormesby cut across the circle, as demonstrated here by an unidentified vehicle.

A view from the shed doorway. No. 6 stands in the yard, displaying an 'On Tow' board in the platform window as No. 3 clicks across the circle. The 'Turning Circle' signs on the rear panels can be clearly seen.

No. 16 crosses the bridge near Cargo Fleet, en route for North Ormesby.

The routes crossed two railway lines. One was adjacent to the depot. No. 2 ascends the ramp. The depot is on the right. The yard seems full of Leyland motorbuses.

In 1965 the bridge needed repairs and was closed. About 600 yards of diversionary wiring was installed, and a level crossing. Seen during installation, a trolley descends the bridge ramp towards the depot.

Number 2 cautiously crosses the railway at the temporary level crossing by the Cargo Fleet end of the Dorman Long works.

Trolley No. 17 edges under the very low railway over-bridge, her trolleys over the pavement. The slopes down to this bridge, the other railway crossing, and the ramps up to that at Cargo Fleet were the only 'hills' on the system.

No. 6 for North Ormesby passes the Whitworth Rd junction opposite Argyle Street. The young lady on the far left sports curlers under her headscarf – a common sight in these times. She's probably got a date for tonight !

At the junction of Normanby Road and Marlborough Road was the most complex piece of overhead, other than at Cargo Fleet.

In the top picture, the nearby reversing triangle is just beyond the trolleybus.

The lower view is looking towards Cargo Fleet.

No. 2 speeds past the railway sidings and Dorman Long's power plant from which TRTB obtained their electricity until 1955.

Heading for Grangetown, No. 6 is about to turn into Birchington Avenue. The Whitworth Road junction is in the far distance.

There were two large roundabouts along Birchington Avenue, the central road of the Grangetown Estate. Although both were quite new, the first had signs of landscaping, framing No. 12.

The other, which formed no part of a road junction – just an obstruction at the time – was bare.

At that time, Grangetown terminus was around another large roundabout at the edge of the estate.

Normanby terminus was another tight turn, very similar to North Ormesby. No. 12 stands in the bay. High Street runs across the photo, behind No. 12. On each photo, note the very economical bus stop on the pole on the left.

No. 6 turns at Normanby. The extension went left from here, along High Street.

TRTB trolleys exhibited this illuminated sign on the rear panel, to warn other motorists of their right-turn antics.

No. 7 speeds along Normanby Road, against a murky background which was a Teesside feature at the time.

What a difference a few trees can make ! No. 12 nears Normanby terminus, on the Grangetown-Normanby extension.

285 in new turquoise livery passes The Miners Arms on High Street. Alas, no miners or trolleys anymore !

Two TRTB tower wagons, one a conversion from a bus, the other rather antiquated, are passed at speed by No. 16 heading for Normanby.

When the Reading system closed Teesside acquired a few of the modern front entrance trolleys. They were repainted in the new TRTB livery. For some reason 291 was decorated for the closure of the system, rather than an original Teesside vehicle.

Sister vehicle 289 was driven on her batteries, and with little ceremony, to the scrap line.

READING

Only two cross-city routes and one other route remained at the time of my visit, but there was still variety in the fleet.

Although rather chaotic in the very centre of town, there were very pleasant open suburbs with well-designed estates and plenty of greenery, and roads were generally quite spacious.

The trolleys were all clean and with a well-kept livery. The only untidiness was the advertising, especially on the front-entrance vehicles.

The routes operating at this time were:

15   Northumberland Avenue to Stations

16   Community Centre to St Mary's Butts

17   Wokingham Road to Tilehurst

18   Liverpool Road to Armour Hill

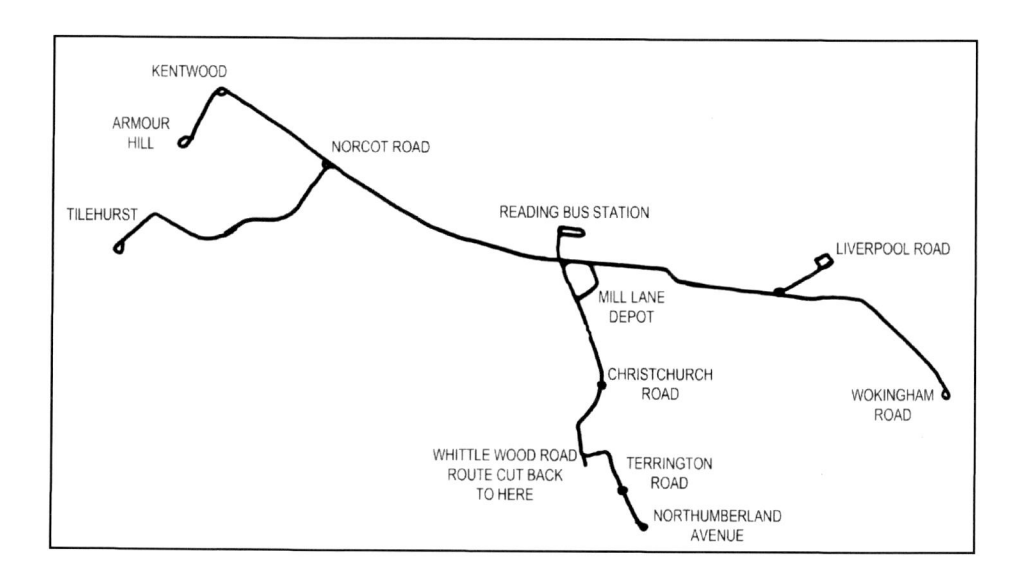

Wokingham Road terminus is just beyond the tree, at the junction with Holmes Road. 155 is about to depart for Tilehurst as 193 arrives at the first stop. The Fire Station is on the right.

183 from Liverpool Road passes the entrance to the cemetery at Wokingham Road junction. A turning facility is provided here for Cemetery short-workings.

The inscription above the former Tramways Power Station.

A peek into Mill Lane Depot. 143, 140 and 182 are lined up ready for service.

183 speeds away towards town from the roundabout at 'The Kentwood'.
She looks rather down on the rear nearside springs !

181 arrives at 'The Kentwood' roundabout. She takes the Armour Hill wires.
The adjacent ones are for the route 18 short- working.

Tilehurst terminus was at the Reading boundary (top of Park lane).
193 prepares to turn.

183 enters the terminus at Armour Hill.

192 on route 17 Wokingham Road takes things steadily along Norcot Road passing the junction with Churchend Lane.

173 passes the War Memorial at Tilehurst, en route for Wokingham Road.

182 passes the 'Battle Inn' in Oxford Road.

155 heads for town. 185 on '18 Armour Hill' passes Waylen Street Post Office.

Northumberland Avenue terminus. 190 has discharged her passengers, and the crew pause for a chat.

190 heads back to the Station, and is seen here negotiating the roundabout at Hartland Road.

190 to Northumberland Avenue holds up a couple of hay wagons in Bridge Street.

147 has run from Community Centre to Broad Street, and now heads for depot via Duke Street.

185 turns to Tilehurst, at the Norcot Road / Oxford Road junction.

Norcot Road terminus, situated where the Tilehurst (to the left) and Armour Hill (to the right) routes diverged. 176 turns, her conductor running behind after pulling the frog.

190 on route 15 leaves Reading Stations loop. The railway station is beyond on the left.

144 turns at St Marys Butts on service 16 to Community Centre, which was the turning circle at the Torrington Road/Northumberland Avenue roundabout.

BOURNEMOUTH

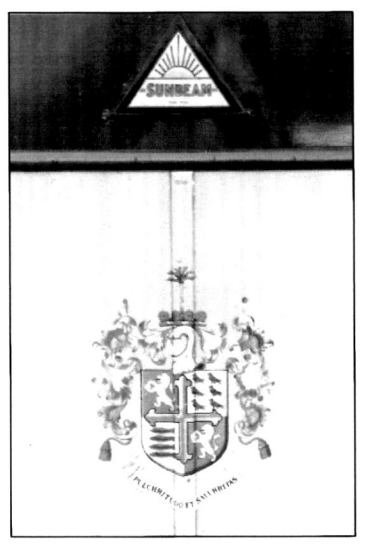

A few days spent here allowed the time to walk all the surviving routes. Not only that but the weather was pleasant too. The smartly turned-out trolleys seemed very much part of this peaceful and tidy town.

Contributing to the smart appearance was the fact that no advertising was carried at the time.

Bournemouth trolleys carried the coat of arms on the front panel, seen here surmounted by the 'Sunbeam' manufacturer's logo.

As a Northerner a downside to Bournemouth was the difficulty of finding decent fish and chips. Haddock? Without bones? Fried in beef dripping? No chance !

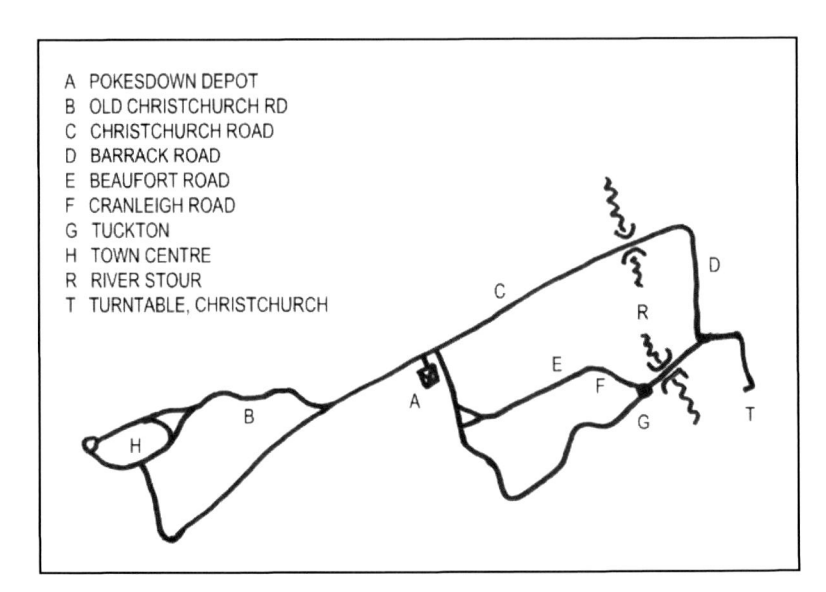

A POKESDOWN DEPOT
B OLD CHRISTCHURCH RD
C CHRISTCHURCH ROAD
D BARRACK ROAD
E BEAUFORT ROAD
F CRANLEIGH ROAD
G TUCKTON
H TOWN CENTRE
R RIVER STOUR
T TURNTABLE, CHRISTCHURCH

Although quite a lot of redundant wiring was still in place, and including that to Mallard Road depot at Strouden, the only routes operating were:

　　　　20 and 21　　　　Bourmenouth to Christchurch
　　　　22 and 23　　　　Bournemouth to Tuckton
　　　　24　　　　　　　　Bournemouth to Jumpers

There were several one-way streets in the town centre. Here we see trolleys 270 (above) and 284 (below) in Gervis Place.

277 turns in to Avenue Road, having rested at The Triangle bus park.

The Square (actually a large roundabout) had multiple wiring. Here 270 on route 22 circles round to join the middle wires from Avenue Road. The wires on the right went to Richmond Hill but were tied off just after the roundabout.

274, outbound on route 20, enters the Lansdowne roundabout.

295, inbound on route 23, leaves the roundabout heading for Bournemouth Square.

Exhibiting a rather battered front panel, 275 performs a merry dance with wayward cars.

One of Bournemouth's ancient tower wagons at Mallard Road. The two poles leaning against the wall, with cables attached, are T-poles. One bar made contact with lowered trolley heads. The other was hooked on the wires, enabling vehicles to be moved several yards away from the wires.

Mallard Road depot housed several trolleybuses for preservation. Two Bournemouth 6-wheelers could be found here, a conventional body double-decker and open top number 202. From 1959, Bournemouth bought only 4-wheel vehicles.

A gaggle of trolleys at Pokesdown Station. The wires straight on go to Jumpers and Barrack Rd. The ones to the right go to Seabourne Road.

Congestion outside Pokesdown depot, the wires to which are on the left. [L-R] 286 on route 23 heads for town; 273 squeezes through to Tuckton. 286 and another have been reversed out of the depot, across the road, and now stand with booms down awaiting their crews.

284 at Tuckton roundabout en route for Christchurch. The wires beyond her come from Cranleigh Road. 284 will now exit to the right of the picture.

277 inbound crosses Tuckton Bridge. The warning sign on the left gives trolleys a maximum speed of 10 mph on the bridge, and forbids two trolleys on at once.

286 on route 23 Tuckton crosses from Beresford Rd to Beaufort Rd. The wires to the right are part of a turning loop for trolleys from Tuckton to Southbourne.

274 on route 23 to Tuckton takes the wires for Beresford Road. The parallel wires lead to Southbourne Grove and Tuckton. The wires to the left of the photo form the Fisherman's Walk turning loop.

299 runs across the circle at the junction of Carbery Avenue and Tuckton Road. This circle was mostly used by the summer-only service 38.

A rare feature on a trolleybus system is the turntable. Bournemouth had one at Christchurch, tucked away in a yard off High Street. Before turning, the negative trolley activated an indicator to warn following vehicles that the yard was occupied. On leaving, the indicator was cancelled, the contact for which can be seen on the left hand wire. Here 274 enters the yard.

Once on the turntable, the booms are hooked down. Two young helpers and the crew will turn 303 by pushing the bus or the two levers provided. The two posts beyond 303 are lights for night-time.

The driver heaves on the lever, and aided by a casual helper, turns 274. The turntable could accommodate a 6-wheel trolleybus.